Missing you

Working your way through loss

By Fay Bloor

Published in the UK by:
Dandelions Bereavement Support
101-111 Macklin Street
Derby
www.wathalls.co.uk

Words by Fay Bloor
www.faybloor.com

Illustrations by Michael Ashley
www.michaelashleyillustration.wordpress.com/

Funding by Wathall's

Design by Gravity Digital

First printed November 2022

ISBN 978-1-3999-3110-6

Thank you to the members of the Dandelions Support Groups for all your help and support in the writing of this book.

I'd like to start by saying how sorry I am, because if you're looking at this book it most likely means that someone you cared for greatly has died.

This book has been designed to hold your hand and guide you through processing this strange and difficult time. Its aim is to reassure you that what you're feeling is ok and, perhaps most importantly, to give you hope that whilst your grief will not end (because your love for that person will not end), it will change and eventually things will, for the most part, feel brighter again.

The thing about grief is that it changes as you work through it over time, new emotions may surface and existing ones may change greatly, or disappear altogether. For this reason, you may want to initially skip parts of this book and come back to them if and when they feel relevant, you may also want to revisit some sections further down the line to acknowledge how things have changed for you. Just as there is no right or wrong way to grieve, there is no right or wrong way to use this book, simply go with what feels the most natural.

Myths around grief

Despite grief being a universal experience, there are a lot of myths and misunderstandings that surround it, perhaps because people often treat death and grief as something to be hidden and not talked about. Here are a few of the most common misconceptions:

• Grief can be avoided

If only this were true. Grief can be pushed aside and ignored for a while, but unfortunately it will not be put off forever. It may be that it takes an increasingly large amount of energy to keep it at bay, or it might come out in different and less healthy ways than if you'd allowed yourself to process it. It's a natural instinct to avoid pain where possible, so it makes sense that we'd want to avoid our grief, or perhaps your situation means you simply don't have a lot of time to grieve, especially if you lead a busy life or have young children to take care of. Unfortunately, keep putting your grief off may lead to you being too exhausted to do all the other things effectively anyway, so it does make sense to consciously set some time aside to work though it.

• Feelings have to be rational

Some of the feelings we have after the loss of a loved one are absolutely not rational, and we can know they are not, but that doesn't make them any less real or powerful, they still need processing and working through with the same amount of care.

• Grief has an end date

Unfortunately grief never ends, but that doesn't mean it remains as it currently is either. Grief will not end because you will always love and miss that person. However, your life will build back up around the loss and, as you work through your feelings over time, you will be able to remember the good times with them with much happiness rather than just the current sadness and pain.

• Not crying means you do not care

Whilst this is obviously not the case, it still deserves a mention because it is something that people can feel guilty about even though they have no control over it whatsoever. Sometimes people are far too shocked to cry at first, even if the death was expected, other times the grief just comes out in different ways, the tears will eventually come if that's what right for you with this particular loss, but if they don't, remember they are not an indication of love.

• There is a 'right' way to grieve

This is absolutely not true, grief is as unique as the individual facing it. Whilst there are a number of common emotions and experiences that people often have after a loss, it doesn't mean you have to go through all these things in order to 'complete' your grieving, they're simply things you might experience. Perhaps because of the well-known models of grief that show the emotional stages in a neat linear progression, it can feel like there is a 'tick list' to grief. Whatever feelings come up for you are absolutely ok for your particular loss, just take them as they come.

• The first year is the most intense

Again, grief is different in each instance and for some people this may well be true, whilst others may feel like they were in a daze for much of the first year and the second year, or even third, is when the loss begins to fully register with them. Don't try and predict how your grief will go, it's impossible and will only put pressure on yourself to fit those expectations, take it as it comes.

• You grieve the same way for every loss

Because grief is so specific to the relationship lost, the way you grieve one loss is likely to be very different to the way you grieve another. How you grieve will depend on a whole number of factors including your personality, your history of loss, what else is happening in your life at the time, your relationship with the person that died and the secondary losses that occur (See page 32).

The person I am missing

Their name was ....

They were my ....

My first memory of them is ....

....

....

Something we liked to do together was ....

....

....

Stick a picture of your loved one on this page, you may want to colour in the frame.

How they died

When did they die? ....

They died because ....

....

....

Did you know they were going to die? ....

How did you find out they had died? ....

....

....

Write about the last time you saw the person before they died. Where were you?
What were you both doing? Is there anything you would change about this memory?

....

....

....

....

....

....

The funeral

Was there a funeral for your loved one? ....

Did you go to the funeral? ....

Did you have a say in the funeral arrangements? ....

Was the funeral as you would have wanted it for them? What made it that way? ....

....

....

....

Do you think the service was a good reflection of their life? ....

....

What was a comforting part of the funeral? ....

....

....

....

....

....

What was a particularly difficult part? ....

....

....

....

....

Emotions of grief

When someone we love dies we are left with a whole host of emotions, though some of them may not appear straight away. It is common in grief to experience a mixture of emotions all at once, even if they are conflicting.

Some of the most common emotions include:

Sadness
Numbness
Guilt
Anger
Worry
Envy
Loneliness

Of course, this list is just an example of what you might feel. You may feel some of the above emotions, all of them, or various different ones. Again, there is no right or wrong way to feel, nor are there positive or negative emotions, as long as you acknowledge the feelings and express them in a healthy way.

The following few pages will look at the emotions listed in slightly more detail and give some ideas of how to deal with them. When we experience strong emotions, it is common to feel physical expressions of them in the body (see points below). Taking note of how these feelings manifest physically can make it easier for you to identify them, which is why the following pages will also ask you to make a note of what they feel like to you and where in the body they appear. It may help to use different colours whilst you do this.

Common physical symptoms of grief:

Knots in stomach
Difficulty swallowing
Breathlessness
Change in appetite
Skin disorders
Shakiness

This list is by no means exhaustive, there are many other feelings that you might experience, can you name any you think are missing? ....

....

Of course, if you are getting physical symptoms and you are concerned, it is worth getting them checked out with your doctor to confirm there is nothing else causing them.

Sadness

Whilst sadness is probably the most predictable emotion to feel after grief, the intensity can still catch us off guard. It can be overwhelming and hard to see a way out of when in the depths of it. Although the intense sadness is uncomfortable whilst it lasts, it does lessen as you begin to process your grief. The pain of the loss will always be there, because you'll always love and miss that person as much, but as your grief moves on, it does change and there is space for life around it.

Use the gingerbread man to show how and where you feel sadness in your body.

Missing them

What do you miss the most about the person?

....

....

....

....

Is there anything you don't miss? (It's ok to say if there is, they were human and therefore not perfect all the time! If you can't think of anything that's ok too, simply move onto the next page).

....

....

....

....

Numbness

It is extremely common, especially in the first few weeks or months after a loss, for it not to seem real. You may know perfectly well in your mind that they are gone, but there is still a part of you that expects your loved one to walk through the door any minute, or for the hospital to call and say it was just a big misunderstanding. This numbness can cause confusion when people expect to be blanketed in deep sadness straight away and it doesn't come. It can also confuse those around us when the numbness wears off and people who thought we were 'over the worst of it' see us getting more upset than when the person first died. The numbness does serve a purpose though, it acts as cushioning to prevent us from becoming overwhelmed by our reaction to the trauma all at once, allowing us to still function.

It is common during this time to experience what is often referred to as 'brain fog', which seems to cloud your thoughts making it difficult to think, remember things or make decisions.

Draw on the gingerbread man what numbness feels like to you.

Breathe

It can be useful to create some space in your mind by practicing mindfulness, as it can help those hidden emotions begin to come through to the surface, allowing you to start processing your grief.

Set aside some time, about 10-15 minutes and find a comfortable place to sit or lay where you will not be disturbed. Read through the following meditation slowly, visualising the feelings in depth. It might help to record yourself slowly reading the meditation so you can close your eyes and listen to it. Do not do the following exercise whilst operating any vehicle or machinery, or if you are anywhere that you will need to stay alert. Remember that mindfulness takes practice, do not worry if your mind starts to wander, simply bring your thoughts back and continue.

When you are ready, begin taking a nice slow, deep breath in and holding for a second or two before slowly releasing. Continue this slow, gentle breathing throughout the exercise. It should feel comfortable, and after a few of these breaths you may already feel yourself beginning to relax.

Bring your attention to the very top of your scalp, imagining a line of relaxing light travelling down your body, relaxing you more and more as it works its way down.

Feel that line of wonderful relaxation travel downwards from your scalp, down over your forehead, gently releasing any tension that may have been held there. Continue down, over your eyebrows, your eyes, down to your cheeks to your jaw. Feel that line of relaxation reach your jaw and any tension release, you may feel your teeth part and your mouth open slightly as this happens, that is ok.

Next feel the relaxation spread down your neck, over your shoulders and slowly down your left arm, reaching right into the very tips of your fingers, which may start to tingle as you focus on them. That wonderful relaxation now travels down your right arm, right down past your elbow and down into the very tips of your fingers which, again, may start to tingle as you focus on them.

That healing line of relaxation now continues through your chest, filling it with gentle, healing warmth before moving on slowly down your spine, right down your back and into your hips, notice that any tension you might have been holding simply drains away leaving you calm and so, so comfortable.

From your hips, feel that wave of relaxation roll down your left thigh, down over your knee, down over your ankle and into your foot, right into the very tips of your toes which, just like your fingers, may start to tingle as you focus on them. Then, feel calmness travel down your right thigh, down over that knee and right down that leg into your foot. Notice the toes on this foot also start to tingle.

You are now completely relaxed from head to toe, take a few moments to breathe and notice how it feels to have released all tension from your body. Some people report feeling a wave-like sensation flowing over their body, this is ok.

Notice any thoughts that pop into your head, try not to interact with them but simply observe them before moving them out of your head again. If you are struggling to clear your mind, simply bring your attention back to your breathing, focusing on the feeling of your chest rising and falling. Continue this way for a few more minutes, observing the thoughts that crop up before allowing them to drift away again.

When you are ready, start to bring some movement back by wiggling your fingers and toes. Then start moving your arms and legs before slowly opening your eyes and sitting or standing up and having a nice stretch, perhaps a sip of water might be refreshing.

To conclude the meditation, contemplate these questions. It's important to remember that there are no right or wrong answers:

How did that feel? ....

....

How easy was it to clear your mind of thoughts? ....

....

Was there a theme to the thoughts that did pop up? ....

....

....

Were you surprised by any of the thoughts you had? If so, which ones? ....

....

....

Guilt

Guilt is an extremely common feature in many people's journey of grief and is usually expressed in "should", "shouldn't have" and "if only" statements. It's important to remember that whilst the cause of these feeling may not always be rational, it doesn't make the emotions involved any less real, or lessen the impact that they have on you.

Grieving people can feel guilty for a whole host of reasons including:

Things they did or did not say

Things they did or not do

Having to put the person in a care home

Not being there when the person died

For falling out with friends or family around the time of death or because of the death

Not telling the person that they loved them enough

Thinking that they should have spent more time with the person

Falling out with the person before they died

Not being able to afford better healthcare

Guilt that they may have somehow caused the death

Not being able to prevent the person dying

There is a big difference between feeling guilty and actually being guilty. Usually in the death of a loved one there is nothing we can do to change the outcome, however much we'd like to. Making ourselves feel guilty gives us the illusion of some sense of control. By imagining how the situation may have been different if we'd somehow acted differently, we feel less powerless.

It is possible that at times that our actions maybe did unintentionally cause hurt or misunderstanding, or perhaps there were a few extra moments here or there that we could have spent with our loved one before they died, but hindsight is a wonderful thing. You loved the person that died, your grief is evidence to that, chances are that you would not intentionally hurt them, or avoid spending as much time with them as possible, whilst still meeting your own needs. If you knew then what you know now maybe you would have acted differently, but unfortunately we don't have that option. It's helpful to remember that you did the best you could, with the knowledge and means you possessed at that time.

Draw on the gingerbread man what guilt feels like to you.

Is there anything you feel guilty about? (If not, simply move onto the next page) ....

....

Are these thoughts rational? (Again, it doesn't make the feeling any less real if not, but it is

helpful to acknowledge.) ....

....

Did you do these things with the intention of hurting anyone or letting anyone down? ....

....

If you could change one thing about the situation, what would you change and why? ....

....

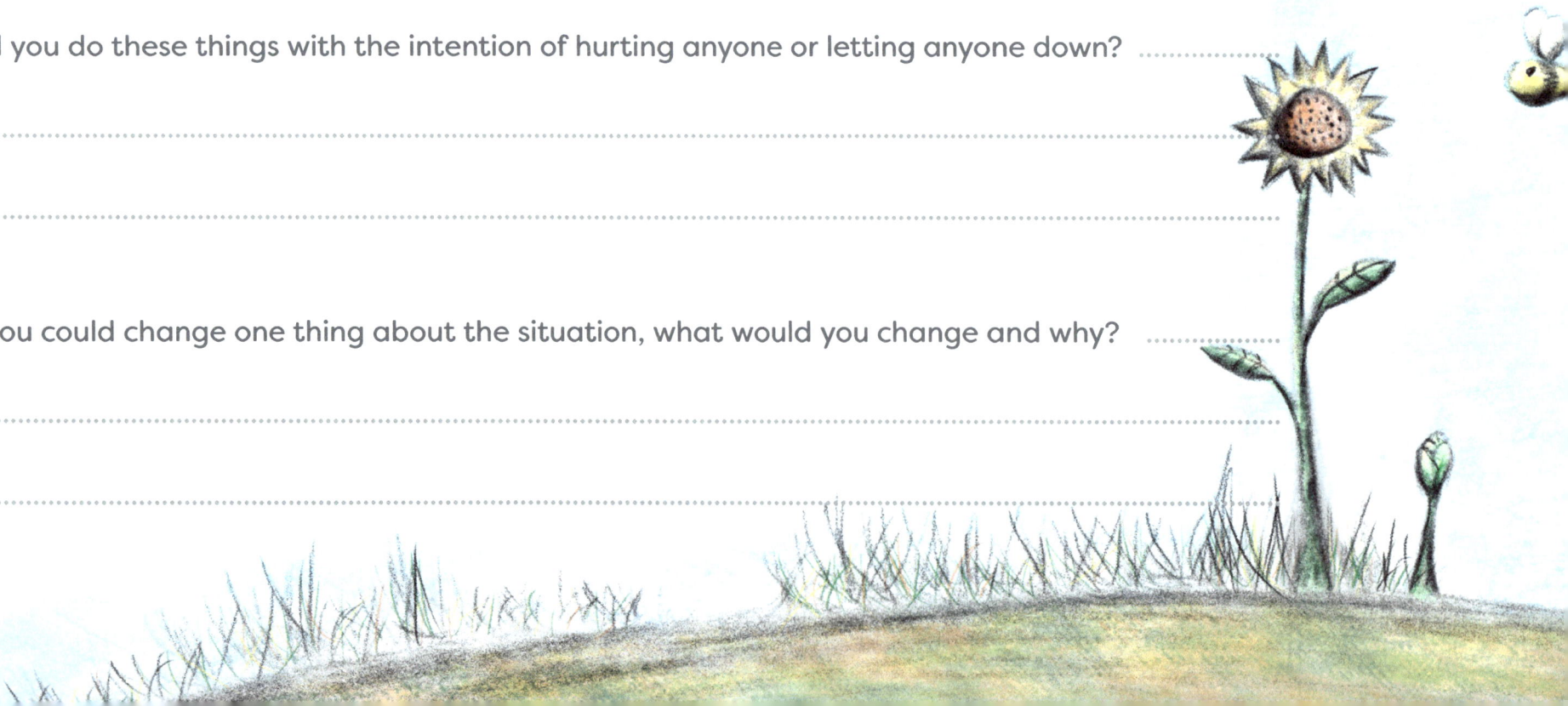

Anger

Anger is a strong and powerful emotion that is extremely common in grief. As a society we tend to view anger as quite a negative emotion related to destructive behaviours, an emotion to shy away from. In reality, anger is a natural and harmless feeling, as long as it is expressed in a healthy way.

In grief anger can be directed in a multitude of directions, including:

Healthcare providers - For any perceived shotcomings, or for something a professional may have said or done.
Family members - Perhaps for not being 'there' or for something they did or did not say or do.
At the person that died - For leaving us, or for not taking better care of themselves, not going to the doctors sooner etc.
At life - For being unfair or for carrying on without that person.

At the situation - We didn't choose to be bereaved, why is this happening to us?
At a higher power such as your god - How could they let this happen? Are they punishing me for something?

And of course, there are many more.

Anger is frequently a front for various other emotions, and spotting which ones underpin yours can be incredibly helpful in diffusing it. Which feelings do you think cause your anger?

....

....

....

....

Draw on the gingerbread man what anger feels like to you.

Who or what do you feel anger at? ....

....

What are you angry at them for? ....

....

Are these feelings rational? (Again, it doesn't make the feeling any less real if not but it is helpful to acknowledge.) ....

....

Do you think they did this with the intention of causing hurt to yourself or others? ....

....

Forgiveness, as well as healthy expression, is the antidote to anger, see page 34 for more on forgiveness.

Worry

When someone we love dies, it's quite natural for us to worry. Our whole world has changed, along with our idea of how we thought life would be. We might find ourselves living on our own, potentially for the first time ever, meaning we now have to worry about managing tasks around the house, or about finances now that person has gone, or perhaps their death has highlighted our own mortality or that of others we love. We tend to think that bad things happen to other people, never to us, so when something bad does happen, we realise that other bad things could also happen, causing us to worry.

Worry also tends to come hand in hand with change, even with what we perceive as positive changes, so it's only natural for you to feel worried in such a time of upheaval and sadness.

What does worry feel like to you? Draw it on the gingerbread man.

What, if anything, is worrying you? Simply move on to the next page if this doesn't feel

relevant. ....

....

....

Is there anything that will make these things feel less worrying? ....

....

....

Is there anyone that can help with these worries? ....

....

....

Mindfulness is a very helpful tool when coping with worry as it helps to calm the mind and give you a break from the barrage of negative thoughts, try the meditation on page 17 to help with your worrying.

Envy

Some of the emotions that pop up in grief can be quite surprising, and envy is one of the feelings that tends to catch people off guard. People expect to feel sad and sometimes to feel angry, but they're not always prepared for the envy of seeing other people that still have their loved one, or even envying the person that died for not having to feel such pain. People can feel quite guilty for being envious of others whose loved ones are still alive, but it's not that you're wishing your pain upon them, you're simply wishing it away from yourself, it's a natural way to feel.

What are some situations that make you feel envious of others? It could be seeing parents doing the school run, seeing couples going about day-to-day life together or maybe special days like Christmas, where everyone is together

with their loved ones..

....

It is important to remember, like we said with anger, envy isn't a negative emotion that you should be ashamed of feeling, it's a natural reaction to a hurtful event. It only becomes negative if you don't express it in a healthy way.

Draw on the gingerbread man what envy feels like to you.

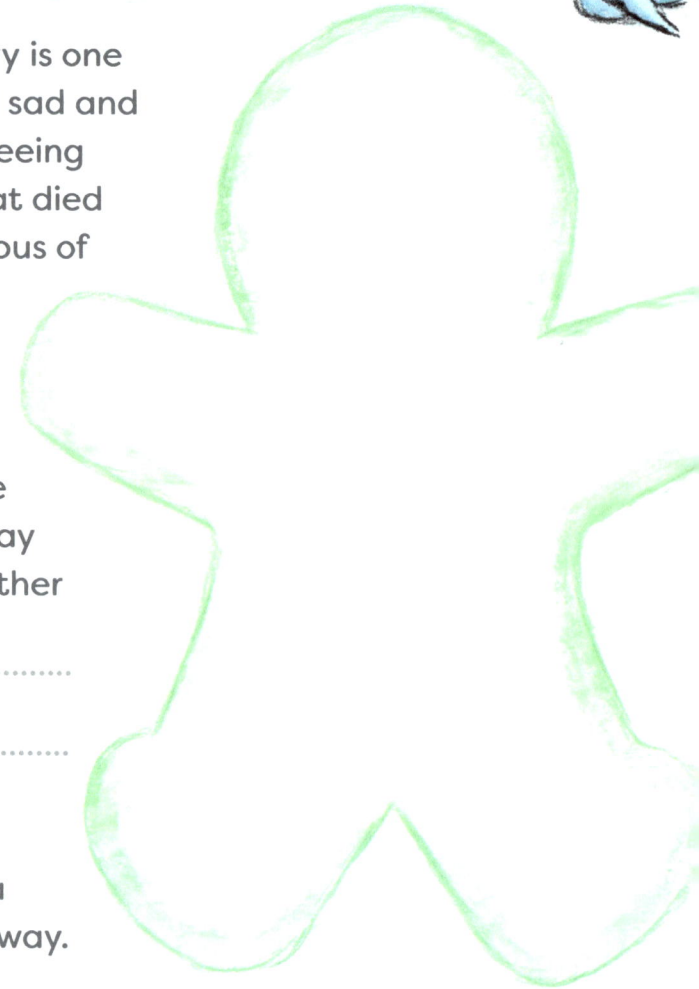

Gratitude

Often the last thing we even think about feeling after the death of a loved one is gratitude, it may feel insulting that I'm even suggesting it, but please bear with me. We cannot change that they have gone, the crater their death has left in our life can be colossal and nothing will fill it, but that isn't to say that everything worthwhile about life has died with them. Exercising gratitude allows you to see the good things, however small, that remain to bring you pockets of joy in even the hardest of days and helps you to cope with the envy at others.

Gratitude Garden

Write something you're grateful for on each flower, you might want to draw some more flowers if there are more things you want to write about. Some things you are grateful for might include good memories with your loved one or the loved ones that are still around you.

Loneliness

Loneliness is a huge part of grief, regardless of who has died and who remains around you. Grief is lonely because only we know exactly how we are feeling, even if we're sharing the same loss with another person, the way we react to the death will have at least some differences. Speaking to others who have experienced the same type of loss, in the same circumstances will likely reveal many similarities and help us to feel understood, but there will still be differences.

Grief is also lonely because we're missing that one specific person, often the one we want to talk to about how we're feeling; all the understanding and kind words in the world will not change the fact that we are missing them and yearning for their presence.

Many people report loneliness to be the hardest part of their grief. It's the least easily remedied and least easily spotted from the outside looking in, especially if you have lots of people around you. Loneliness is not simply cured by having people around, in fact it can often cause us to push people away, rather than have to put on a front and pretend we're ok whilst around them.

How does loneliness feel to you? Draw it on the gingerbread man.

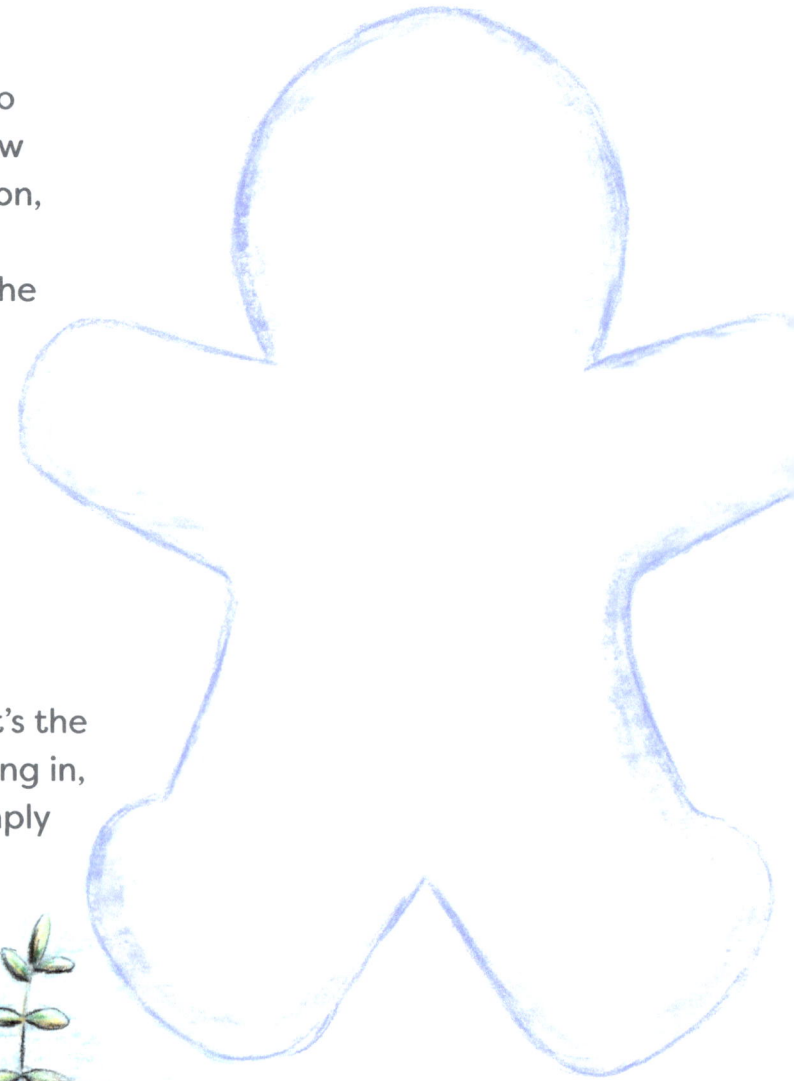

Are there certain times of day that you feel most lonely? ....

....

....

Are there certain situations that you feel most lonely in? ....

....

....

Are there certain people you feel more lonely around? ....

....

....

Is there anything you can do or ask for that would help with these feelings? ....

....

What else has been lost?

When someone close to us dies our whole life changes, even aspects that you would expect not to be touched by the loss seem to feel different. This is because of **Secondary Losses**, losses that have occurred as a direct result of the initial loss. Secondary losses can be anything from the person that does the DIY around the house, to the loss of your role, to the loss of your dreams for the future.

Secondary Losses

On the opposite page write down as many **Secondary Losses** that you can think of that are relevant to your situation, to get you started there are some examples for each category below.

- **Social Losses**
  Friendship groups - Sometimes change after a death if people don't know what to say or if you always went out as couples etc.
  Someone to attend events with.

- **Practical Losses**
  Having to learn to manage the finances.
  The person that drives.

- **Physical Losses**
  Cuddles.
  Someone to come home to.

- **Identity Losses**
  Loss of your role as a carer.
  Do you still consider yourself to be married/a parent?
  (No right or wrong answers here).
  Plans you had for the future.

What Secondary Losses have you experienced since your loved one died?

Social Losses

....

....

....

....

Physical Losses

....

....

....

....

Practical Losses

....

....

....

....

Identity Losses

....

....

....

....

Forgiveness

Forgiveness is frequently misunderstood as something you do for someone else. It's often thought that by forgiving someone, you're letting them off the hook or saying that what they did is acceptable. This isn't true, you don't have to forget what they did, or feel ok about it, and the person doesn't even have to know you've forgiven them. Forgiveness is something you do for **you**, it disperses those gnawing feelings inside you and instead helps to bring you peace and relinquish the power that the person's actions have over you. Look back at your gingerbread men for Anger and Guilt, are the sensations you've drawn pleasant? Chances are, they're feelings you'd rather not have. Forgiveness isn't easy, but it's essential to moving forward with your grief and maintaining a healthy mindset. Failure to forgive puts strain on your body and can lead to bitterness, potentially damaging your other relationships.

How to forgive

Forgiveness can be a tricky thing to achieve, it forces you to face your hurt head on, and then release it out. Forgiveness is a process, it's not something people can usually do straight away. It also has to be deliberate, if someone has done something that has really hurt you, or you feel you've done something that needs forgiving, it's unlikely that you'll just wake up one day feeling ok about it, the first step is to decide to forgive, even if the person is not sorry. Secondly, you need to acknowledge the emotions, when someone has hurt us we don't simply feel anger or pain, there are a whole myriad of feelings that can be triggered by the person's actions, all of which underpin the grudge you are holding. Take the time to observe your feelings, why do you think those specific emotions are the ones that have come up? Unearthing, acknowledging and understanding feelings is vital to releasing them.

Who do you need to forgive and why? ....

....

....

What feelings underpin your anger at the person? ....

....

....

Why do you think those specific feelings have come up? ....

....

....

Try writing a letter that you don't intend to send to the person that needs your forgiveness (even if it's to yourself). Detail what they did, how that made you feel, including the feelings that underpin your anger. Finish the letter by saying that you chose to forgive them and let go of any bad feeling for your own sake. It can be therapeutic to (safely) burn or rip up the letter afterwards as a 'letting go' ritual.

Journaling

Journaling, or the act of writing out your thoughts and feelings, has widely been hailed as a powerful coping mechanism for various difficulties and the same is true in grief, it helps by:

Being a non-judgemental outlet for you to release the intense feelings that come with grief in to.

Helping you to identify patterns in your thoughts and feelings, which in turn can help you identify grief triggers.

Helps you to identify some of the practical problems that grief can cause, and possible solutions for them.

It can help you to see how far you've come in your grief. On difficult days it can be hard to remember a time when things didn't seem so bleak. Looking back through your journal can remind you that not every day is as hard as this one feels, and eventually you'll notice that the tricky days come further and further apart.

Being constantly available. Often grief wakes us in the middle of the night with our minds working overtime, or won't let us go to sleep in the first place. However good your friends are, frequently calling them in the middle of the night isn't really a viable option. Your journal is great for emptying your head into in the middle of the night, calming your mind and helping you to drift off. It can be worth keeping it by your bed with a pen for this reason.

If you've never journaled before it can be hard to know where to start, in truth there is no right or wrong way to do it, just go with what feels right and helpful to you, but here are some tips to set you on your way:

• Get a journal that speaks to you, there are lots of layout and design options out there and it's important to find one that feels right for you. There is something vastly therapeutic about putting pen to paper when writing about your emotions, but if it isn't for you there are also journaling apps available, many of which can be passcode protected.

• Mix up the style to suit your mood. There are many different styles of journaling, there's the traditional writing about your day and feelings journal, but this can also be done by colouring the page with shades that match your emotions for that day. Gratitude journals – writing down a set number of things you're grateful for each day, even on bad days can help to shift to a more positive mindset. You can even use the journal to write 'letters' you don't intend to send, either to the person that has died or perhaps someone you need to forgive. Mix up the style to fit your needs at the time, it's there to help you so go with what feels right.

• Write quickly to prevent you critiquing your thoughts or altering them to what you think they 'should' be. No one else is going to see your journal, it doesn't need to be perfect and edited, it doesn't even have to make sense, it just needs to give you an outlet.

Memories

Our memories are important until someone we love dies, and then they become essential. For many people they can be hard to face at first, the good memories taunt us about what we've lost, the difficult memories around the death are too raw and intrude without warning. As we process the grief over time, the hurt around both types of memory settles, and we can see more than just the pain. The good memories remind us that our loved one is not just someone that died, they're someone that lived, and who made memories and connections with others. The good memories put their life in perspective of their death.

What are some difficult memories of your loved one?

....

....

....

....

....

What makes them particularly hard?

....

....

....

....

....

What are some good memories?

....

....

What's your favourite memory of them and why?

....

....

....

....

....

....

....

Rituals

A ritual can be defined as a ceremonial act or action, something that we do to mark an occasion or situation. In grief we tend to have many rituals, especially if you follow a religion, many of which are steeped in tradition. A funeral is a prime example of this, a chance to mark the passing of a loved one and acknowledging their life, using memories, readings and symbolism.

There is safety in the traditions of rituals, often people don't know how they're 'supposed' to act or be in the wake of a loss, the rituals provide a safe harbour in the tumultuous sea of emotion, providing protection and direction for the bereaved.

It can be hard for people when, for whatever reason, they cannot make the funeral, or if there is no funeral at all, as it takes away the ritual and thus the protection it provides. Even if they can go to the funeral, often people find comfort in continuing rituals on special days, or just on the days they miss that person the most, to acknowledge their ongoing love and grief.

Thankfully ritual is something we can create for ourselves wherever we are, and whenever we wish. There is a whole spectrum of what can be considered a ritual, but at its heart it just needs to be something you can do meaningfully to help you honour that person. Ideas include:

Lighting a candle in memory of them – perhaps you have a special one that you use specifically for this purpose

Wearing a piece of their clothing or jewellery to special events or on special occasions, to keep them close on the day.

Reading a poem or meaningful reading at their place of rest, or perhaps somewhere you used to enjoy going together.

Laying flowers somewhere for them.

Journaling or scrapbooking memories of them.

Creating a memory box for them containing photos, written memories and items that remind you of them.

Planting something or creating a work of art in their memory.

There are no right or wrong ways to use ritual, and this list is by no means exhaustive. Listen to what feels right for you, you'll instinctively know what you want, even if it takes a little bit of time to think of it.

Things left unsaid

Even if we know that someone is dying and we have all the time we need to say goodbye, there is almost always still something we wished we could have told them. It could be to tell them again how much you loved them, to tell them how much you miss them, or to tell them what's been happening since you last saw them. Writing letters to your loved one can be a powerful way to keep your bond with them, and help get those messages off your chest. Use these pages to write a letter to your loved one. You can always use an extra sheet of paper if you need more room.

Dear ....

....

....

....

....

....

Kindness

Kindness can be a powerful tool to help you work through the loss of your loved one, making the world a brighter place whilst you're at it. Extending kindness to ourselves and others gives us the chance to live our lives in a way we know our loved ones would be proud of, and is a positive outlet for the love we would have shown to them.

Random acts of kindness are little acts that you do for others, to make their days a little bit easier or brighter, with no expectation of reward or payoff, simply for the purpose of making their day better. The magical thing is, the more you extend kindness, the better you feel.

Think about the last time you did something nice for someone else. What was it, how much effort did it cost you and how did it make you feel?

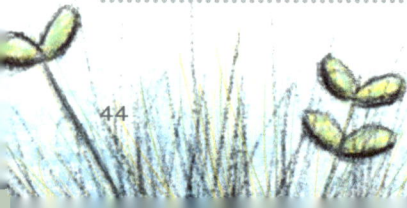

Random Acts of Kindness inspiration

There are countless ways to share kindness with others, most of which cost very little effort whilst still making both of your days that little bit brighter. The idea is to just spread a little kindness to others, whether you know them or not, which often encourages others to go on and do the same, and so on. Remember to take care of yourself whilst being kind to others and to set boundaries to protect yourself. Some ideas for random acts of kindness are:

Holding the door for someone

Sending a letter, text or email to a friend or relative you've not been in touch with for a while

Smiling at someone

Donating unneeded items or spare change to a good cause

Volunteering your time for a worthwhile cause

If you think something nice about someone, tell them

Letting the person behind you at the shop with only a couple of items go first

Many, many others

Over the next few weeks the act of kindness I will try and fit into each week is:

....

....

....

....

How did you feel when you performed that act of kindness?

....

....

....

....

Acceptance

When we talk about acceptance in grief, we don't mean feeling good or fine about the loss. We mean it in terms of taking stock of where you are now, gathering up your courage and strength, and working towards where you want to be, in life as you now find it. Even if, to start with, that simply means stepping up to the extra roles left to you, or dragging yourself out of bed on the tricky days. Acceptance in grief is about taking responsibility for your own wellbeing and position in life. It's the "OK, this is where I find myself - what can I do about it?".

Control

Hand in hand with acceptance comes control. Looking at what we can control and having the courage to do so, whilst letting go or putting aside that beyond our reach. Of course, this is easier said than done when we're weathering the storm of our emotions. Below are some examples of things inside and outside of our control, to help to differentiate.

Things I cannot control:

The past
Other people's actions
What other people think
Mistakes made by others
Illness
External events

Things I can control:

My actions
My boundaries
What I think
My choices
Learning from mistakes
Whether I ask for help

What is upsetting you right now? List all the things, big or small. (You may want some extra paper to do this on).

-   •

-   •

-   •

Looking over your list, how many of these things can you control? Those you cannot are the things you can mentally put aside. If you can control them, what are you planning to do about them?

It might feel therapeutic to cross out (or if you've used separate paper, cut out and throw away) those beyond your control.

Has this made a difference to your list? Does it feel as daunting as when you first wrote and looked at it? Are there any action plans that can be drawn for the items within your control? If you can do something, do you need to?

....

....

....

....

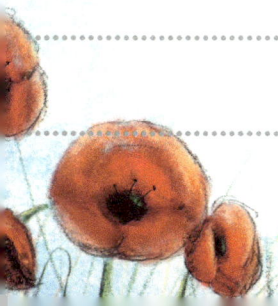

Self-Care

As we've mentioned, grief is hard work. It drains us emotionally and physically, and leaves us feeling like we're treading water, trying to keep our head above the surface. It's vitally important that we practice self-care as we go along our grief journey, to help us maintain emotional and physical resilience.

When we're in the throes of a tough day, it can be hard to remember the things that help during a tough day, so these pages are here to serve as a reminder of the things to reach for, and the things to avoid when the intense feelings of grief set in. It goes without saying that the things that help should all be used in moderation. As for the things that bring you down, of course only avoid the things that you reasonably can, and even then only temporarily.

Things that make me feel better when I'm having a hard day (Can be as small as a nice cup of tea, a bubble bath or a walk in nature) are:

....

....

....

....

....

....

....

....

Things that bring me down, even on a good day (household jobs, negative people) are:

....

....

....

....

....

....

....

Things I wish I'd known about grief

Whilst things are slowly starting to change, there is still a strange taboo around death which prevents people honestly sharing their experiences with others, leaving people feeling shocked and isolated when it happens to them. The wonderful members of our Dandelions Bereavement Support groups have been kind enough to share the things they wish they'd known about grief and loss, rawly and honestly, in the hope that it helps others feel less alone.

"The way that it completely consumes you; puts a full stop on your life. It gives you a new set of values; makes you appreciate things more. Close friends do not know what to say to you. Utter loneliness, no one to share troubles with."

"After losing my wife I was kept busy for a while dealing with the admin work that followed her death and it was not until that work was completed that I started to feel the reality of Anne's absence!"

"Rituals with others are very important to the process of saying goodbye."

"Some people, who are kind and mean well, are embarrassed by a bereaved person show emotion."

"I wish I'd known that it doesn't always mean immediate sadness. I remember feeling bad for smiling and being happy about other things after he had died."

"When the search for a stem cell donor failed to source a match, warning bells should have rung but if they did I didn't want to hear them! I did become aware that treatment options were now very much reduced and in time the Leukaemia began to regain the upper hand. Treatment continued but of course this impacted upon her immune system and infections became a regular occurrence up to the one which finally took her away from us on 19th April 2019. I wish I had been prepared for losing my wife, but I hoped against hope that I would not have to. We do not rehearse losing someone who we love, do we?"

"Caring friends are a great help and comfort."

"How hard it would be having to write 'widow' on forms as marital status, feelings like the marriage certificate was no longer valid and not knowing what to do with my wedding ring – should I still wear it?"

"How much music can evoke tears or sadness, particularly if your partner enjoyed it or maybe you danced together to it."

"That I'd feel so uncomfortable and like an outsider at events attended mainly by couples."

"It is very comforting when someone takes a true interest and shows care for your situation."

"Things that feel impossible at the start become possible as time goes on."

"Grief can continue in a healthy way, it doesn't have to end."

"When you have lost your husband/wife, it still feels lonely even when you are surrounded by your own family."

"Despite being able to talk to family and friends and/ or go out during the day and evening, I only became aware of intense loneliness when I put down the telephone after the last conversation of the day or returned home to the empty house. How I wish I could have been prepared for that!"

"I wasn't prepared for the pain of seeing couples together, and the envy that I would feel."

"Sorrow is a very important thing to be felt, shared and addressed without Shame."

"What took me by surprise in the immediate few days after my partner died is the physical pain in my chest."

Is there anything you would add here?

....

....

....

....

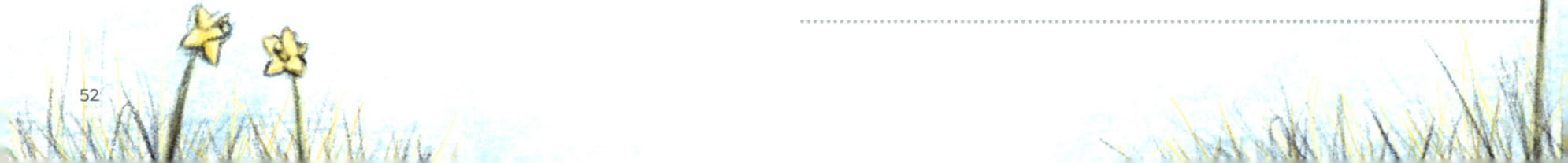

Reflection

What are the most noticeable changes you've observed within yourself since your loss?

Has anything surprised you? ....

....

Have you learnt anything new about yourself? ....

....

Have you learnt anything new about those around you? ....

....

....

Have you learnt anything new about life because of the loss? ....

....

....

My Support Network

The people we can trust to talk to and who
will help take care if us when we are having a bad
day are known as our Support Network.

Who is in your Support Network? Write their names on
the dandelion seeds below. Add some extra seeds if you
need to.

The next time you feel down, pick someone from your
support network to talk to about it. If they also loved
the person that died, they might feel a similar way.

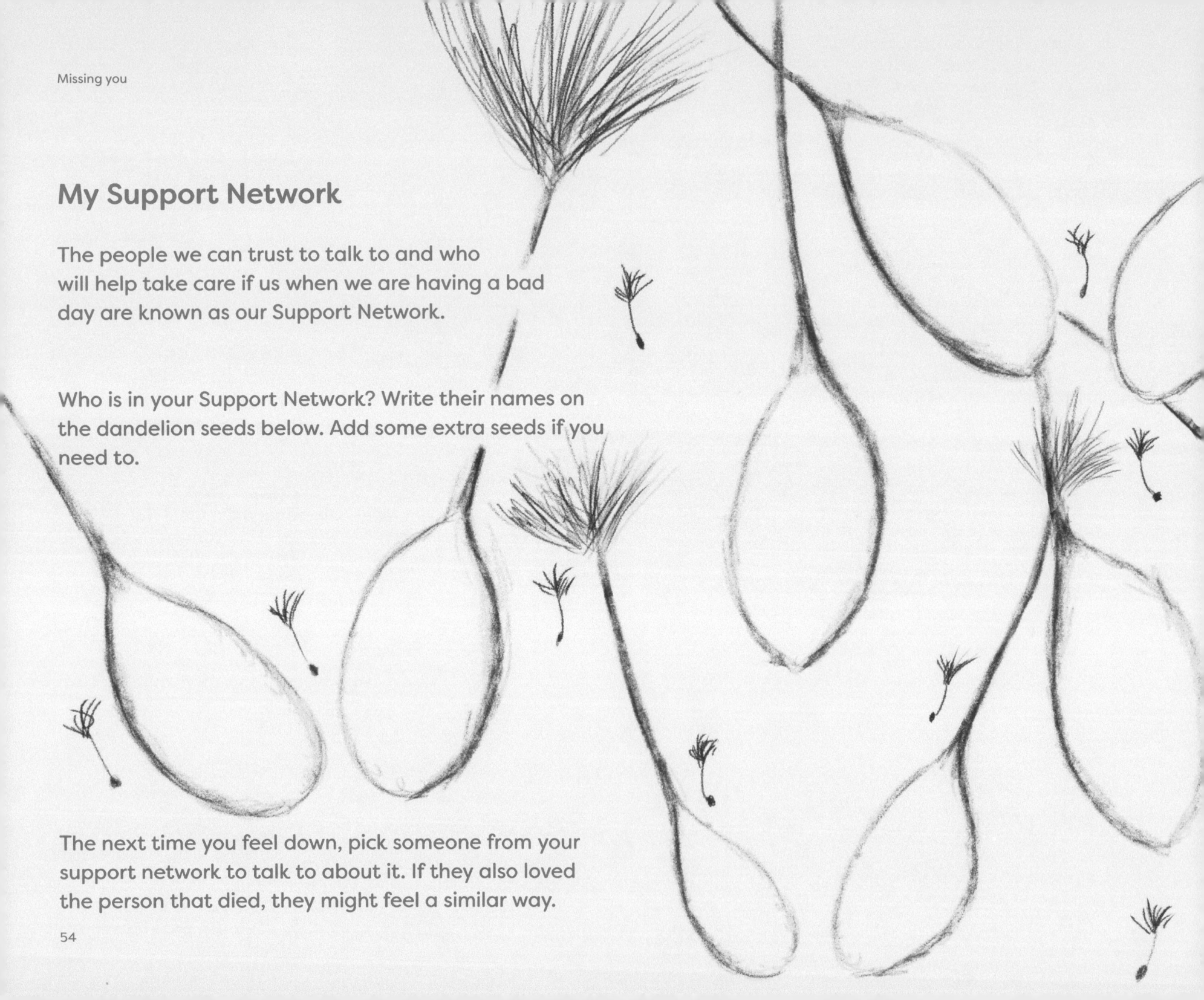

Goodbye

This brings us to the end of the book, hopefully it's been useful as you face and work through life as it now is. Whilst the book has ended, your grief continues, constantly changing. Look after yourself and refer back as and when you need to, always remembering that it's normal – and fine – to have good days and bad, and to flit between emotions.

I cannot stress enough the importance of talking and being heard, it validates your feelings and allows you to feel seen. Please do be brave enough to reach out to friends or support groups and find the listening ears you both need and deserve.

Grief is an unfortunate complication of love, but also proof that love endures.

ISBN 978-1-3999-3110-6

9 781399 931106

90000

In association with:

Wathall's
WITH YOU SINCE 185

www.ingramcontent.com/pod-product-compliance
Lightning Source LLC
Chambersburg PA
CBHW041554030426

42337CB00005B/52